Charles Ditlefse

Those MAGNIFICENT TRAINS ®

2 0 0 2 D A T E B O O K

Front cover: Milwaukee Road Boxcab Freight Motor No. E36B is on an eastbound freight at Butte, Montana, on October 8, 1956.

Photo by Fred Herson

Back cover: Southern Pacific narrow gauge Ten-Wheeler No. 9 works a short freight on the Keeler branch in the Owens Valley of California on August 21, 1959.

Photo by John Hungerford

CEDCO

PUBLISHING

Copyright © 2001. All rights reserved.
Cedco Publishing Company
100 Pelican Way
San Rafael, CA 94901
www.cedco.com

A CSX loaded eastbound coal train is at Providence Forge, Virginia, in February 1989.

Photo by Kurt Reisweber

JANUARY

MONDAY	TUESDAY
	1
	New Year's Day

WEDNESDAY	THURSDAY
2	**3**
New Year's Holiday (N.Z. & Scotland)	

FRIDAY	SATURDAY
4	**5**
	Last Quarter Moon ☾

SUNDAY	
6	

An ancient Nevada Copper Belt gas-electric, the *Yerington*, crosses the Mokelumne River, on the Central California Traction Company, in January 1978.

Photo by Alan Miller

JANUARY

MONDAY 7	**TUESDAY** 8
WEDNESDAY 9	**THURSDAY** 10
FRIDAY 11	**SATURDAY** 12
SUNDAY 13	

New Moon ●

Led by its burgundy colored Alco FA's, the *Napa Valley Wine Train* passes the Sunny St. Helena Winery, on its southbound return trip to Napa, on March 17, 1990.

Photo by Alan Miller

JANUARY

MONDAY 14	**TUESDAY** 15
WEDNESDAY 16	**THURSDAY** 17
FRIDAY 18	**SATURDAY** 19
SUNDAY 20	

Santa Fe Nos. 50 and 50B, a DL-109 A and B, are at the Argentine, Kansas, yard on May 18, 1957. Built for Santa Fe's fast passenger trains, they were not up to the job. They were downgraded to local service out of Kansas City and were retired early.

Photo from the Al Chione collection

JANUARY

MONDAY
21

Martin Luther King Jr. Day
Wellington Anniversary (N.Z.)
First Quarter Moon ☽

TUESDAY
22

WEDNESDAY
23

THURSDAY
24

FRIDAY
25

SATURDAY
26

Australia Day (Aust.)

SUNDAY
27

JANUARY-FEBRUARY

MONDAY
28

Auckland Anniversary (N.Z.)
Full Moon ○

TUESDAY
29

WEDNESDAY
30

THURSDAY
31

FRIDAY
1

SATURDAY
2

SUNDAY
3

FEBRUARY

MONDAY

4

Nelson Anniversary (N.Z.)
Last Quarter Moon ☽

TUESDAY

5

WEDNESDAY

6

Waitangi Day (N.Z.)

THURSDAY

7

FRIDAY

8

SATURDAY

9

SUNDAY

10

Norfolk & Western Y class 2-8-8-2 No. 2158 is the pusher on an eastbound coal drag on this sunny day in May 1955.

Photo by John Hungerford

FEBRUARY

MONDAY	TUESDAY
11	**12**
	Lincoln's Birthday
	New Moon ●

WEDNESDAY	THURSDAY
13	**14**
Ash Wednesday	St. Valentine's Day

FRIDAY	SATURDAY
15	**16**

SUNDAY

17

Southern Pacific's Bicentennial GP40P-2 departs San Francisco's 4th Street Station with a Christmas Eve Special in 1975.

Photo by Gary Vielbaum

FEBRUARY

MONDAY

18

Presidents' Day

TUESDAY

19

WEDNESDAY

20

First Quarter Moon ◐

THURSDAY

21

FRIDAY

22

Washington's Birthday

SATURDAY

23

SUNDAY

24

Conrail No. 6852 disturbs the peace of the tiny hamlet of Lockwood, New York. Located on the Ithaca Secondary, the town sees a steady stream of covered hoppers carrying coal and rock salt between Ithaca, New York, and Sayre, Pennsylvania.

Photo by Bruce Fingerhood

FEBRUARY-MARCH

MONDAY

25

TUESDAY

26

WEDNESDAY

27

THURSDAY

28

Full Moon ○

FRIDAY

1

SATURDAY

2

St. David's Day (Wales)

SUNDAY

3

Seaboard Air Line E7A No. 3032, with the help of an E4A, leads Passenger, Mail, and Express train No. 3 on its southbound trek from Washington, D.C., to Birmingham, Alabama. No. 3 is at Raleigh, where it is scheduled for a 25 minute stop, from 3:55 to 4:20 p.m.

Photo by Wiley Bryan

MARCH

MONDAY

4

Labour Day (W.A.)

TUESDAY

5

Last Quarter Moon ☽

WEDNESDAY

6

THURSDAY

7

FRIDAY

8

International Women's Day

SATURDAY

9

SUNDAY

10

Mothering Sunday (U.K.)

MARCH

MONDAY

11

Eight Hours Day (Tas.)
Taranaki Anniversary (N.Z.)
Commonwealth Day (U.K.)
Labour Day (Vic.)

TUESDAY

12

WEDNESDAY

13

New Moon ●

THURSDAY

14

FRIDAY

15

SATURDAY

16

SUNDAY

17

St. Patrick's Day

MARCH

MONDAY

18

TUESDAY

19

WEDNESDAY

20

THURSDAY

21

Vernal Equinox 2:16 P.M., E.S.T.

First Quarter Moon ◗

FRIDAY

22

SATURDAY

23

SUNDAY

24

Palm Sunday

Just placed in service after a major rebuild is California Western No. 46, a handsome 2-6-6-2 Mallet. It previously worked for the Rayonier Lumber Company as No. 111. Now its duties include the *Super Skunk* passenger trains of the California Western, as seen on this September day in 1970.

Photo by Tom Moungovan

MARCH

MONDAY
25

Otago Anniversary (N.Z.)

TUESDAY
26

WEDNESDAY
27

THURSDAY
28

Passover
Full Moon ○

FRIDAY
29

Good Friday

SATURDAY
30

SUNDAY
31

Easter
Daylight Saving Time begins (United Kingdom)

A Southern Railway northbound freight is headed for Alexandria, Virginia, in July 1984. The train is seen on the Tye Bridge near Lynchburg.

Photo by Kurt Reisweber

APRIL

MONDAY

1

Easter Monday (Aust., Canada, N.Z., Rep. of Ireland & U.K.)

TUESDAY

2

WEDNESDAY

3

THURSDAY

4

Last Quarter Moon ☽

FRIDAY

5

SATURDAY

6

SUNDAY

7

Daylight Saving Time begins (Canada & U.S.)

Union Pacific No. 6936, the railroad's last operating *Centennial* locomotive, or DD40X, leads an Engineering Department inspection train around the famed Tehachapi Loop in Southern California, on April 15, 1999.

Photo by Elrond Lawrence

A P R I L

MONDAY

8

TUESDAY

9

WEDNESDAY

10

THURSDAY

11

FRIDAY

12

SATURDAY

13

New Moon ●

SUNDAY

14

Nickel Plate Road No. 803 leads a train of mixed freight at Adena, Ohio, on June 16, 1955.

Photo by Bill Price

APRIL

MONDAY
15

TUESDAY
16

WEDNESDAY
17

THURSDAY
18

FRIDAY
19

SATURDAY
20

First Quarter Moon ☽

SUNDAY
21

APRIL

MONDAY

22

Earth Day

TUESDAY

23

St. George's Day (Engla

WEDNESDAY

24

THURSDAY

25

ANZAC Day (Aust. & N

FRIDAY

26

National Arbor Day
Full Moon ○

SATURDAY

27

SUNDAY

28

APRIL-MAY

MONDAY

29

TUESDAY

30

WEDNESDAY

1

THURSDAY

2

FRIDAY

3

SATURDAY

4

Last Quarter Moon ◑

SUNDAY

5

Lima Locomotive Works built some really attractive Shays, perhaps none more so than construction number 3233, the former Mt. Emily Lumber Company No. 1. This 80-3 class engine now makes her home on the City of Prineville Railway in Central Oregon.

Photo by Tom Moungovan

MAY

MONDAY
6

May Day Holiday (Rep. of Ireland & U.K.)
Labour Day (Queensland)

TUESDAY
7

WEDNESDAY
8

THURSDAY
9

FRIDAY
10

SATURDAY
11

SUNDAY
12

Mother's Day (Aust., Canada, N.Z. & U.S.)
New Moon ●

Louisville & Nashville E8A No. 5794, in its original paint scheme, leads an excursion train at Nashville in April 1997. The unit began life on the Pennsylvania Railroad and was acquired by the Tennessee Central Railway Museum.

Photo by Alan Miller

MAY

MONDAY
13

TUESDAY
14

WEDNESDAY
15

THURSDAY
16

FRIDAY
17

SATURDAY
18

SUNDAY
19

Pentecost
Whitsunday (U.K.)
First Quarter Moon ☽

Painted in the red, white, and blue of the *American Freedom Train*, ex-Southern Pacific No. 4449 leads the AFT through Arlington Heights, Illinois, on August 4, 1975. This was the first outing for the 4-8-4 in its new paint scheme.

Photo by Larry Kostka

MAY

MONDAY	TUESDAY
20	21

Victoria Day (Canada)

WEDNESDAY	THURSDAY
22	23

FRIDAY	SATURDAY
24	25

SUNDAY

26

Full Moon ○

Nevada Northern No. 40, a beautiful little 4-6-0 Ten-Wheeler, leads a two car passenger special on the desert of Nevada near East Ely, in November 1958.

Photo by John Hungerford

MAY-JUNE

MONDAY

27

Memorial Day (observed)
Spring Holiday (U.K.)

TUESDAY

28

WEDNESDAY

29

THURSDAY

30

FRIDAY

31

SATURDAY

1

SUNDAY

2

Last Quarter Moon ☾

JUNE

MONDAY

3

Queen's Birthday (N.Z.)
Holiday (Rep. of Ireland)

TUESDAY

4

WEDNESDAY

5

THURSDAY

6

FRIDAY

7

SATURDAY

8

SUNDAY

9

J U N E

M O N D A Y

10

Queen's Birthday (Aust. except W.A.)
New Moon ●

T U E S D A Y

11

W E D N E S D A Y

12

T H U R S D A Y

13

F R I D A Y

14

Flag Day

S A T U R D A Y

15

S U N D A Y

16

Father's Day (Canada, U.K. & U.S.)

Union Pacific's 9000 class steam locomotives were the largest solid frame (non-articulated) steam locomotives ever built, with a wheel arrangement of 4-12-2. These locomotives did not go around sharp curves. Here we see No. 9014 sitting at Fremont, Nebraska, on September 2, 1952.

Photo by Jack Pfeifer

JUNE

MONDAY 17	**TUESDAY** 18
First Quarter Moon ☽	
WEDNESDAY 19	**THURSDAY** 20
FRIDAY 21	**SATURDAY** 22
Summer Solstice 9:24 A.M. E.D.T.	

SUNDAY

23

Southern Pacific No. 9236 leads a westbound freight exiting tunnel No. 6 at Norden, at the summit of Donner Pass, in Northern California, on August 31, 1975. Donner Lake is visible just beyond the train.

Photo by Gordon Glattenberg

JUNE

MONDAY	TUESDAY
## 24	## 25

St. Jean Baptiste Day (Quebec)
Full Moon ○

WEDNESDAY	THURSDAY
## 26	## 27

FRIDAY	SATURDAY
## 28	## 29

SUNDAY

30

Norfolk & Western No. 611 is southbound on the former Southern Railway, crossing the Tyger River, near Lyman, South Carolina, on May 1, 1983.

Photo by Kurt Reisweber

JULY

MONDAY
1

Canada Day (Canada)

TUESDAY
2

Last Quarter Moon ☽

WEDNESDAY
3

THURSDAY
4

Independence Day

FRIDAY
5

SATURDAY
6

SUNDAY
7

Southern Pacific Cab-Forward No. 4211 takes water at an unknown location in the Tehachapi Mountains of Southern California, on November 29, 1956. It was built by Baldwin in 1946 as class AC-10.

Photo by John Hungerford

JULY

MONDAY
8

TUESDAY
9

WEDNESDAY
10

THURSDAY
11

New Moon ●

FRIDAY
12

SATURDAY
13

Holiday (N. Ireland)

SUNDAY
14

JULY

MONDAY	TUESDAY
15	16

WEDNESDAY	THURSDAY
17	18

First Quarter Moon ◑

FRIDAY	SATURDAY
19	20

SUNDAY

21

JULY

22

23

24

25

Full Moon ○

26

27

28

Florida East Coast Railway E3A No. 1004 is on the point on train No. 5, *The South Wind*, at West Palm Beach, Florida, on October 29, 1960.

JULY·AUGUST

MONDAY

29

TUESDAY

30

WEDNESDAY

31

THURSDAY

1

Last Quarter Moon ◑

FRIDAY

2

SATURDAY

3

SUNDAY

4

Maine Central U18B No. 408 and GP38 No. 258 sit near the turntable of the Portland Terminal Roundhouse in Rigby Yard, at South Portland, Maine, in April 1976.

Photo by Robert A. LaMay

AUGUST

MONDAY

5

Holiday (Rep. of Ireland & Scotland)·
Civic Holiday (Canada except Quebec)

TUESDAY

6

WEDNESDAY

7

THURSDAY

8

New Moon ●

FRIDAY

9

SATURDAY

10

SUNDAY

11

Southern Pacific Geep No. 5472 leads a westbound freight past the station at Glendale, California, in 1956. Train No. 805 is heading for Tehachapi Loop and Northern California, over the San Joaquin line.

Photo by Gordon Glattenberg

AUGUST

MONDAY

12

TUESDAY

13

WEDNESDAY

14

THURSDAY

15

First Quarter Moon ☽

FRIDAY

16

SATURDAY

17

SUNDAY

18

Led by F3A No. 44C, Santa Fe's *Chief* prepares to depart Chicago's Dearborn Station for Los Angeles in June 1970.

Photo by Robert A. LaMay

AUGUST

19

20

21

22

Full Moon ○

23

24

25

AUGUST-SEPTEMBER

MONDAY

26

Late Summer Holiday (U.K.)

TUESDA

27

WEDNESDAY

28

THURSDA

29

FRIDAY

30

Last Quarter Moon ☽

SATURDA

3

SUNDAY

1

Father's Day (Aust. & N.Z.)

SEPTEMBER

MONDAY

2

Labor Day (Canada & U.S.)

TUESDAY

3

WEDNESDAY

4

THURSDAY

5

FRIDAY

6

New Moon ●

SATURDAY

7

Rosh Hashanah

SUNDAY

8

Grandparent's Day

William Ritter Lumber Company Shay No. 19 is loading logs at Lilly Fork, West Virginia, on June 30, 1960.

Photo by Bill Price

SEPTEMBER

MONDAY	TUESDAY
9	10

WEDNESDAY	THURSDAY
11	12

FRIDAY	SATURDAY
13	14

First Quarter Moon ☽

SUNDAY

15

Southern Pacific's brand new SD-70's Nos. 9818 and 9816 lead the WCRBM train eastbound through Sims, in the Sacramento River Canyon, below Dunsmuir, California, on August 7, 1994.

Photo by Dick Dorn

SEPTEMBER

MONDAY	**TUESDAY**
# 16	# 17
Yom Kippur	
WEDNESDAY	**THURSDAY**
# 18	# 19
FRIDAY	**SATURDAY**
# 20	# 21
	Full Moon ○
SUNDAY	
# 22	

Led by No. 5809, a Central Vermont freight passes "old mills" at Willimantic, Connecticut, in September 1992.

Photo by Robert A. LaMay

SEPTEMBER

MONDAY

23

Autumnal Equinox 12:56 A.M. E.D.T.
Canterbury (South) Anniversary (N.Z.)

TUESDAY

24

WEDNESDAY

25

THURSDAY

26

FRIDAY

27

SATURDAY

28

SUNDAY

29

Last Quarter Moon ◑

Western Pacific No. 3549 leads Burlington Northern train No. 139 as it slides through Virginia in the Feather River Canyon. The train originated in Seattle and is bound for Stockton, California, on September 19, 1979.

Photo by Dick Dorn

SEPTEMBER-OCTOBER

MONDAY
30

Queen's Birthday (W.A.)

TUESDAY
1

WEDNESDAY
2

THURSDAY
3

FRIDAY
4

SATURDAY
5

SUNDAY
6

New Moon ●

OCTOBER

MONDAY

7

Labour Day (A.C.T., N.S.W. & S.A.)

TUESDAY

8

WEDNESDAY

9

THURSDAY

10

FRIDAY

11

SATURDAY

12

SUNDAY

13

First Quarter Moon ☽

OCTOBER

MONDAY	**TUESDAY**
## 14	## 15
Columbus Day (observed) Canadian Thanksgiving Day	
WEDNESDAY	**THURSDAY**
## 16	## 17
FRIDAY	**SATURDAY**
## 18	## 19

SUNDAY

20

Central Vermont 2-8-0 Consolidation No. 454 certainly does not get high marks for aesthetics. She is on the North Local at Palmer, Massachusetts, on October 12, 1954.

Photo by Mike Usenia

OCTOBER

MONDAY

21

Full Moon ○

TUESDAY

22

WEDNESDAY

23

THURSDAY

24

FRIDAY

25

Hawke's Bay Anniversary (N.Z.)

SATURDAY

26

SUNDAY

27

Daylight Saving Time ends (Canada, U.K. & U.S.)

June 3, 1962 finds Pennsylvania GG1 No. 4932 pulling away from the North Philadelphia Station on its run from New York to Washington, D.C. The GG1's will always be remembered for their speed and reliability in all kinds of weather.

Photo by Larry Kostka

OCTOBER-NOVEMBER

MONDAY

28

Labour Day (N.Z.)
Holiday (Rep. of Ireland)

TUESDAY

29

Last Quarter Moon ☽

WEDNESDAY

30

THURSDAY

31

Halloween

FRIDAY

1

All Saints' Day (U.K.)

SATURDAY

2

SUNDAY

3

Santa Fe FP-45 No. 100 leads the westbound *El Capitan* at Raton, New Mexico, on March 3, 1968. These locomotives went through many reincarnations and served well into the 1990s.

Photo by Al Chione

NOVEMBER

MONDAY
4

Marlborough Anniversary (N.Z.)
New Moon ●

TUESDAY
5

Election Day
Guy Fawkes Day (U.K.)

WEDNESDAY
6

THURSDAY
7

FRIDAY
8

SATURDAY
9

SUNDAY
10

Remembrance Sunday (U.K.)

Monon E-unit No. 207 leads northbound train No. 6, *The Thoroughbred*, coming through Salem, Indiana, on October 17, 1964.

Photo by Tom Smart

NOVEMBER

MONDAY

11

Remembrance Day (Aust., Canada & U.K.)
Veterans' Day
First Quarter Moon ◐

TUESDAY

12

WEDNESDAY

13

THURSDAY

14

FRIDAY

15

Canterbury (North & Central) Anniversary (N.Z.)

SATURDAY

16

SUNDAY

17

NOVEMBER

MONDAY	TUESDAY
18	19
	Full Moon

WEDNESDAY	THURSDAY
20	21

FRIDAY	SATURDAY
22	23

SUNDAY

24

NOVEMBER-DECEMBER

MONDAY 25	**TUESDAY** 26
WEDNESDAY 27 Last Quarter Moon ☽	**THURSDAY** 28 Thanksgiving Day
FRIDAY 29	**SATURDAY** 30 St. Andrew's Day (Scotland) Hanukkah

SUNDAY

1

A collage of trains and tracks features Chicago & Eastern Illinois No. 1406 ready to leave Dearborn Station in Chicago, with the *Hummingbird* in July 1955. A beautiful pair of Erie E-units are to the right.

Photo from the Al Chione collection

DECEMBER

MONDAY

2

Westland Anniversary (N.Z.)

TUESDAY

3

WEDNESDAY

4

New Moon ●

THURSDAY

5

FRIDAY

6

SATURDAY

7

SUNDAY

8

The Sierra Railroad's No. 38, a powerful little 2-6-6-2, works a freight train between Jamestown and Oakdale, California, on January 7, 1955.

Photo by John Hungerford

DECEMBER

MONDAY

9

TUESDAY

10

WEDNESDAY

11

THURSDAY

12

First Quarter Moon ☽

FRIDAY

13

SATURDAY

14

SUNDAY

15

Conrail's Office Car Special heads north along the Hudson River, at Bear Mountain, New York, on January 16, 1988. This piece of railroad now belongs to CSX after the 1998 break up of Conrail.

Photo by Howard Ande

DECEMBER

MONDAY

16

TUESDAY

17

WEDNESDAY

18

THURSDAY

19

Full Moon ○

FRIDAY

20

SATURDAY

21

Winter Solstice 8:15 P.M. E.S.T.

SUNDAY

22

GP40 No. 9660 leads Canadian National train No. 393 on the Grand Trunk Western at Brighton, Vermont. It's late afternoon now, but it will be well after dark before it reaches its destination at Montreal.

Photo by Gordon Smith

DECEMBER

MONDAY	TUESDAY
23	24

WEDNESDAY	THURSDAY
25	26
	Boxing Day (Aust., Canada, N.Z. & U.K.)
	St. Stephen's Day (Rep. of Ireland)
Christmas	Last Quarter Moon ☽

FRIDAY	SATURDAY
27	28

SUNDAY

29

Cedco would like to wish you all the best in the coming year.

www.cedco.com

DECEMBER-JANUARY

MONDAY
30

TUESDA
3

WEDNESDAY
1

THURSDA

New Year's Day

FRIDAY
3

SATURDA

SUNDAY
5

NOTES

NOTES

NAME

ADDRESS/PHONE

NAME

ADDRESS/PHONE

NAME

ADDRESS/PHONE

NAME

ADDRESS/PHONE

NAME

ADDRESS/PHONE

NAME   ADDRESS/PHONE

NAME

ADDRESS/PHONE

NAME

ADDRESS/PHONE

WEB SITES

SITE _____

URL _____

PASSWORD CLUE_____

NOTES _____

_____

SITE _____

URL _____

PASSWORD CLUE_____

NOTES _____

_____

SITE _____

URL _____

PASSWORD CLUE_____

NOTES _____

_____

SITE _____

URL _____

PASSWORD CLUE_____

NOTES _____

_____

SITE _____

URL _____

PASSWORD CLUE_____

NOTES _____

_____

SITE _____

URL _____

PASSWORD CLUE_____

NOTES _____

_____

SITE _____

URL _____

PASSWORD CLUE_____

NOTES _____

_____

SITE _____

URL _____

PASSWORD CLUE_____

NOTES _____

_____

WEB SITES

SITE _____
URL _____
PASSWORD CLUE_____
NOTES _____
_____

SITE _____
URL _____
PASSWORD CLUE_____
NOTES _____
_____

SITE _____
URL _____
PASSWORD CLUE_____
NOTES _____
_____

SITE _____
URL _____
PASSWORD CLUE_____
NOTES _____
_____

SITE _____
URL _____
PASSWORD CLUE_____
NOTES _____
_____

SITE _____
URL _____
PASSWORD CLUE_____
NOTES _____
_____

SITE _____
URL _____
PASSWORD CLUE_____
NOTES _____
_____

SITE _____
URL _____
PASSWORD CLUE_____
NOTES _____
_____

WEB SITES

Site _____
URL _____
Password clue_____
Notes _____
_____

Site _____
URL _____
Password clue_____
Notes _____
_____

Site _____
URL _____
Password clue_____
Notes _____
_____

Site _____
URL _____
Password clue_____
Notes _____
_____

Site _____
URL _____
Password clue_____
Notes _____
_____

Site _____
URL _____
Password clue_____
Notes _____
_____

Site _____
URL _____
Password clue_____
Notes _____
_____

Site _____
URL _____
Password clue_____
Notes _____
_____

WEB SITES

Site _____
URL _____
Password clue _____
Notes _____
_____

Site _____
URL _____
Password clue _____
Notes _____
_____

Site _____
URL _____
Password clue _____
Notes _____
_____

Site _____
URL _____
Password clue _____
Notes _____
_____

Site _____
URL _____
Password clue _____
Notes _____
_____

Site _____
URL _____
Password clue _____
Notes _____
_____

Site _____
URL _____
Password clue _____
Notes _____
_____

Site _____
URL _____
Password clue _____
Notes _____
_____

WEB SITES

SITE _____
URL _____
PASSWORD CLUE_____
NOTES _____
_____

SITE _____
URL _____
PASSWORD CLUE_____
NOTES _____
_____

SITE _____
URL _____
PASSWORD CLUE_____
NOTES _____
_____

SITE _____
URL _____
PASSWORD CLUE_____
NOTES _____
_____

SITE _____
URL _____
PASSWORD CLUE_____
NOTES _____
_____

SITE _____
URL _____
PASSWORD CLUE_____
NOTES _____
_____

SITE _____
URL _____
PASSWORD CLUE_____
NOTES _____
_____

SITE _____
URL _____
PASSWORD CLUE_____
NOTES _____
_____

WEB SITES

Site _____

URL _____

Password clue_____

Notes _____

_____

Site _____

URL _____

Password clue_____

Notes _____

_____

Site _____

URL _____

Password clue_____

Notes _____

_____

Site _____

URL _____

Password clue_____

Notes _____

_____

Site _____

URL _____

Password clue_____

Notes _____

_____

Site _____

URL _____

Password clue_____

Notes _____

_____

Site _____

URL _____

Password clue_____

Notes _____

_____

Site _____

URL _____

Password clue_____

Notes _____

_____

SPECIAL DATES

DATE	OCCASION

SPECIAL DATES

DATE	OCCASION

SPECIAL DATES

DATE	OCCASION

PERSONAL INFORMATION

GENERAL
NAME _____
ADDRESS _____
PHONE_____ FAX _____ OTHER_____
COMPANY NAME _____
ADDRESS _____
PHONE_____ FAX _____ OTHER _____

IN CASE OF EMERGENCY
NAME _____ RELATIONSHIP _____
PHONE_____ WORK_____ OTHER_____
ADDRESS _____
NAME _____ RELATIONSHIP _____
PHONE_____ WORK_____ OTHER_____
ADDRESS _____

MEDICAL
PHYSICIAN _____ PHONE _____
PHYSICIAN _____ PHONE _____
DENTIST _____ PHONE _____
INSURANCE/HMO _____ POLICY _____

AUTOMOBILE
INSURANCE CO. _____ POLICY _____
AGENT_____ PHONE _____
DRIVER'S LICENSE# _____ EXP. DATE _____
PLATE# _____ EXP. DATE _____

LOST OR STOLEN CREDIT CARD
CARD_____ PHONE _____
CARD_____ PHONE _____
CARD_____ PHONE _____

IMPORTANT NUMBERS

PUBLIC SERVICES
LIBRARY _____

POST OFFICE _____

PUBLIC TRANSPORTATION _____

PARKS AND RECREATION _____

FINANCIAL SERVICES
BANK/CREDIT UNION _____

BANK/CREDIT UNION _____

CREDIT CARD SERVICES _____

CREDIT CARD SERVICES _____

ACCOUNTANT/FINANCIAL PLANNER _____

MORTGAGE COMPANY _____

HOME SERVICES
LANDLORD _____

PROPERTY MANAGER _____

UTILITIES COMPANY _____

UTILITIES COMPANY _____

LAWN CARE SERVICE _____

WATER COMPANY _____

SANITATION SERVICES _____

CABLE COMPANY _____

NEWSPAPER DELIVERY _____

PLUMBER _____

ELECTRICIAN _____

TELEPHONE COMPANY _____

HOMEOWNERS' INSURANCE AGENT/POLICY _____

PERSONAL SERVICES
HAIRDRESSER _____

DRY CLEANER _____

TRAVEL AGENT _____

VIDEO STORE _____

VETERINARIAN _____

CHILD-CARE PROVIDER _____

MECHANIC _____

SCHOOL _____

NOTES